20p

D0358628

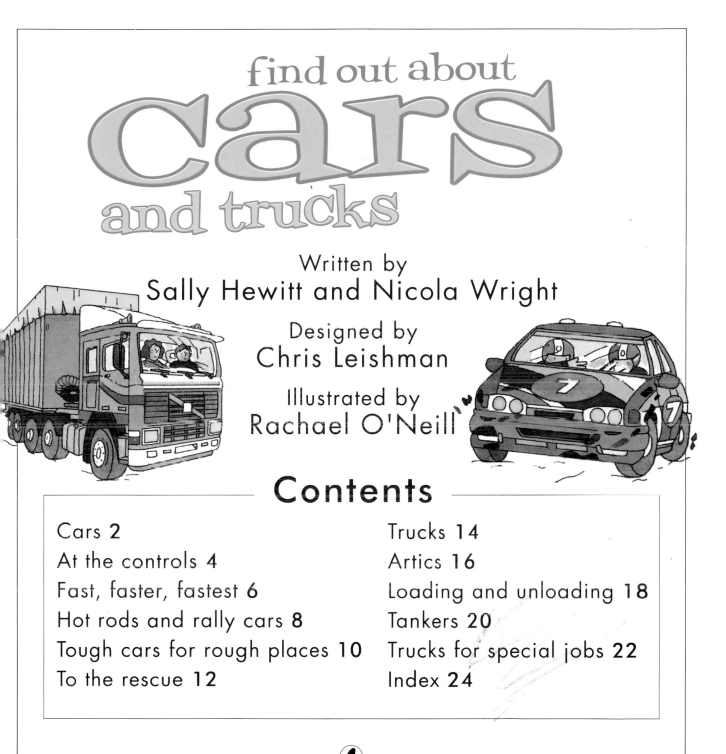

find out about
cars
and trucks

Written by
Sally Hewitt and Nicola Wright

Designed by
Chris Leishman

Illustrated by
Rachael O'Neill

Contents

Chrysalis Children's Books

Cars

Cars come in hundreds of shapes and sizes to suit all the different ways that people use them.

Convertible

Door mirror

Engine

Bonnet

Bumper

Windscreen

Estate

Tyre

Fun Fact

A car has over 14,000 pieces.

Boot

Saloon
Exhaust pipe

Tailgate

Hatchback

Petrol cap

Radiator grill

Types of car

Convertibles have tops that fold back.

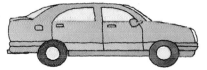

Estate cars have a large space in the back for luggage.

Saloon cars have two or four doors and a boot.

Hatchbacks have a door at the back that opens upwards.

3

At the controls

Cars are complicated machines but the controls to drive them are quite simple.

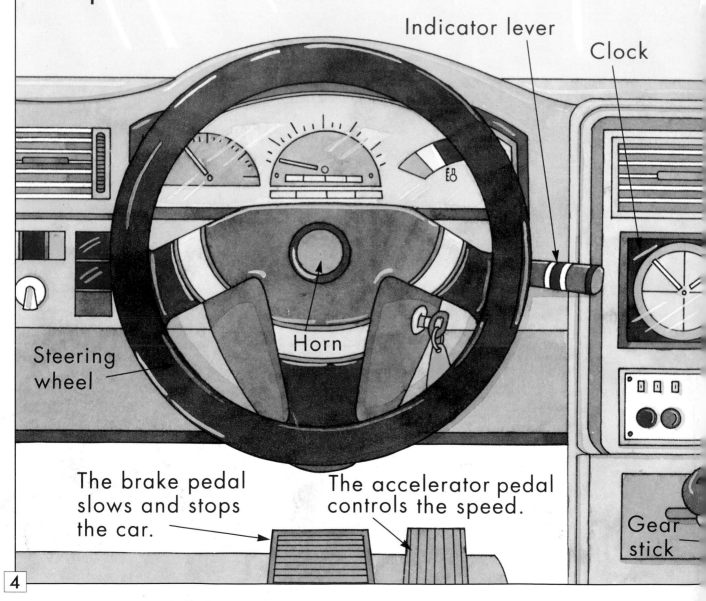

Indicator lever

Clock

Horn

Steering wheel

The brake pedal slows and stops the car.

The accelerator pedal controls the speed.

Gear stick

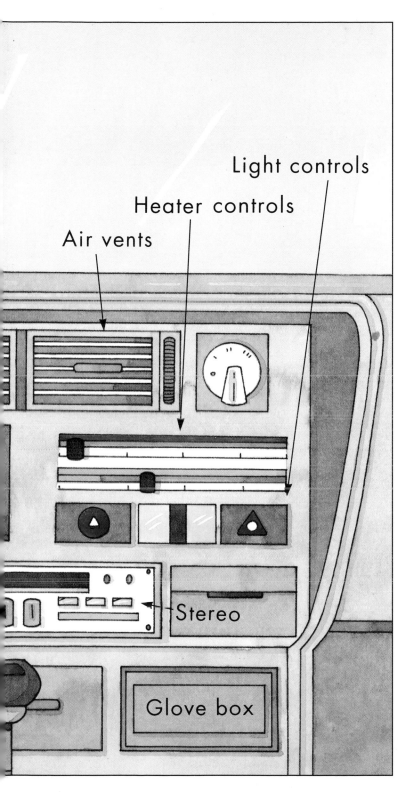

Light controls

Heater controls

Air vents

Stereo

Glove box

Control panel

The dials and lights on the control panel give the driver important information.

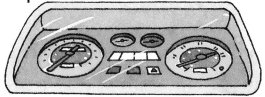

The **low level fuel warning light** comes on when the car needs more petrol.

The **temperature dial** warns when the engine is overheating.

The **speedometer** shows how fast the car is going.

Fast, faster, fastest

Sports cars have powerful engines and streamlined shapes so that air can pass over them easily.

Turbo engine

Streamlined shape

Spoiler

Fun Fact

Speeding racing cars go so fast that sometimes they almost take off! Aerofoils (spoilers) attached to the car act like upside-down wings, keeping the tyres on the ground.

Formula One racing cars are built for one thing – to win races! There is just enough room inside for the driver.

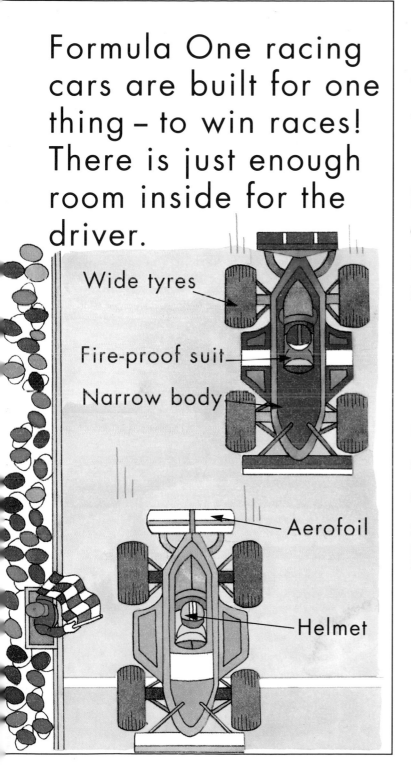

Wide tyres

Fire-proof suit

Narrow body

Aerofoil

Helmet

Built for speed

Slicks Smooth wide tyres called slicks give racing cars extra speed.

Light bodies Racing cars have bodies made of extra-light material.

Powerful engines and lots of gears drive racing cars at speeds up to 400 km/h (250 mph).

Hot rods and rally cars

Hot rods and dragsters are sprinters. They run in drag races. The winner is the fastest to the finishing line – only $\frac{1}{4}$ of a mile away from the start!

Hot rods

Spoiler

Cage to protect the driver.

Dragster

Drag strip

Slick-tread tyres

Rally cars are long distance racers. They run in races that last for days, or even weeks or months.

Fun Fact
The longest rally race ever run was from London to Sydney – 31,107 km (19,329 miles).

Dragsters go so fast that they need **parachutes** to help slow them down.

Rally drivers have a **navigator** in the car to tell them which way to go.

Tough cars for rough places

Tough cars, called off-road vehicles, are built to bump over rocky ground and splash through water. They can go up steep hills and keep a tight grip on downhill slopes.

On the farm

Outdoor pursuits

On safari

Special features

Ground clearance

The bottom of the car is high to clear rocks and bumps.

Tyre tread

Deep tyre patterns, called tread, grip slippery or sandy ground.

Four-wheel drive

All four wheels are powered by the engine. If any of the wheels gets stuck, the other wheels can still work.

11

To the rescue

Police cars, fire engines and ambulances are fitted with special equipment to deal with emergencies. Sometimes they all work together.

Radio

Fire Engine

Hose

Police car

Ambulance

Stretcher

Doing their jobs

Emergency vehicles use blue **flashing lights** and loud **sirens** to warn other drivers to pull over so they can get past.

An **aerial ladder platform** can rescue  people from the top of buildings, down cliffs and under bridges.

Ambulances have **medical equipment** inside to give patients treatment on the way to hospital.

Trucks

Trucks carry and deliver loads all over the country and abroad. They have different shaped bodies for the kinds of loads they carry.

Door mirrors set wide for extra vision.

Box body
A removal truck carries furniture in its box body.

Curtain-sider
The curtains keep the load dry and in place.

Clips

Drop-sider
The sides of this truck can be dropped down to unload the scaffolding.

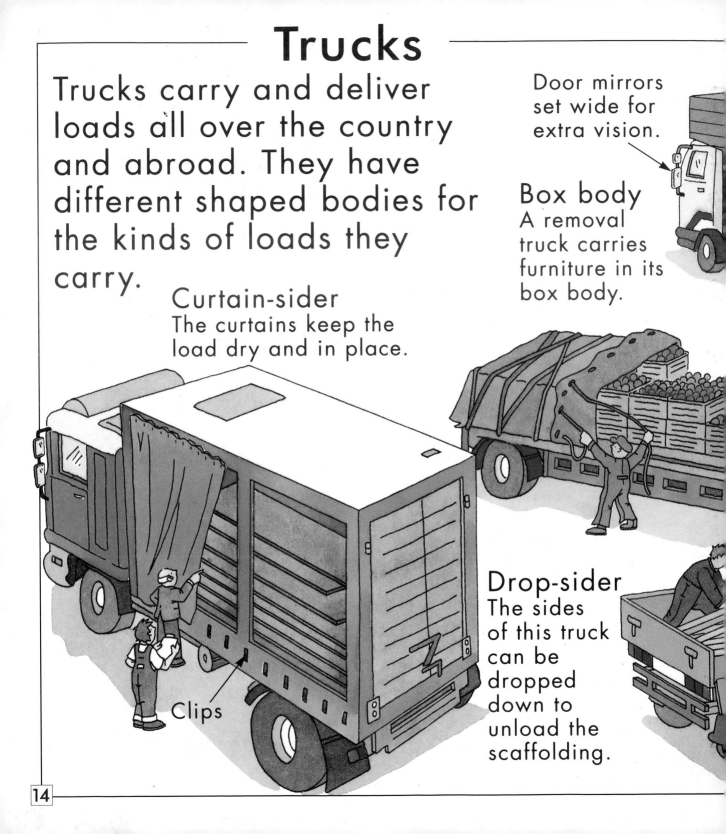

Roll-up door

Flatbed body
It is easy to reach the load once the sheeting and ropes are untied.

Truck parts

Straight trucks have two sets of wheels. Sometimes the back wheels are in pairs.

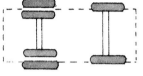

Chassis The chassis is the frame of the truck.

Axle Each set of wheels is on an axle.

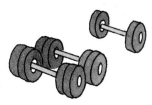

Artics

Articulated trucks, or artics, have two parts – the tractor at the front and the trailer at the back. Tractors can drive without a trailer, but trailers cannot go anywhere without a tractor.

Air deflector

Horns

Trailer

Airlines

Engine

Lights

Heavy trucks often have more than six pairs of wheels.

Cab

Tractor

Cab tilt The cab can be tilted for the driver to check the engine.

Night cab Long distance drivers sleep in a night cab.

Air **lines** are plastic pipes that carry air for the brakes in the trailer.

Loading and unloading

Different loads need special trucks to move them.

A loading machine fills the tipper with buckets of earth.

Some trucks are fitted with cranes for lifting their heavy loads.

A fork-lift truck can load boxes right into the top of another truck.

The middle and top platforms of a car transporter tip to make ramps for driving cars on and off.

On and off

Crane The crane can lift, swing round and lower its head.

Forks Fork-lift trucks have a two-pronged fork which slots into special wooden loading pallets.

Tipper A rod behind the driver's cab opens like a telescope to tip the truck up.

Tankers

Tankers carry liquid loads such as petrol, chemicals and milk. They can also carry powder and granules.

Milk float

Petrol tanker
Petrol is pumped from the petrol tanker into tanks under the forecourt of the service station.

Weighbridge

Gauge

Delivery pipe

Underground storage tank

Silo

Milk tankers

Milk tankers collect milk from farms and deliver it to the dairy.

Petrol pumps

Forecourt

Loads

Dry loads Tankers can tip up to empty dry loads.

Liquid loads are delivered through a pipe.

Dangerous loads have warning stickers. In an accident, a code tells the rescue workers what is in the tanker.

3YE 1270

Trucks for special jobs

Some trucks are fitted with machinery for doing special jobs.

Road sweeper

A brush whirls round cleaning and sweeping.

A giant vacuum pipe sucks up the dirt and leaves.

Snow plough

Strong headlights are needed to work in blizzards.

A spreader swirls salt and grit on to the road to stop it icing up again.

A blade scrapes and pushes snow and ice off the road.

Refuse truck

The back section lifts up and the rubbish is tipped out at a disposal site.

Rotating blades crunch up the rubbish.

Plastic bins are emptied into the truck.

Ultra-heavy hauler

These trucks carry enormous loads. An extra truck is often needed to push from behind or to pull from the front.

A **police escort** with flashing lights and sirens travel with the load to warn other drivers.

Index

Edited by Nicola Wright & Dee Turner
Series concept Tony Potter
Design Manager Kate Buxton
Printed in China

ISBN 1 84138 655 3

10 9 8 7 6 5 4 3 2 1

This edition first published in 2003 by
Chrysalis Children's Books
The Chrysalis Building, Bramley Rd, London W10 6SP

Copyright © Chrysalis Books PLC